HOW TO DEBATE

ROBERT E. DUNBAR

HOW TO DEBATE

FRANKLIN WATTS I 1987
NEW YORK I LONDON I TORONTO I SYDNEY
A LANGUAGE POWER BOOK

Library of Congress Cataloging-in-Publication Data

Dunbar, Robert E.
How to debate.

(A Language power book)
Bibliography: p.
Includes index.
Summary: An introduction to debating, including
preparation and research of a topic, finding
evidence, attacking opposing arguments, and giving
an effective delivery.
1. Debates and debating—Juvenile literature.
[1. Debates and debating] I. Title. II. Series.
PN4181.D86 1987   808.53   86-23353
ISBN 0-531-10335-8

To "Loquacious," who
has matured into
an effective debater

Diagrams by Vantage Art

Photographs courtesy of:
The Bettmann Archive: p. 15;
UPI/Bettmann Newsphotos: pp. 18, 36, 37, 80;
Rothco Cartoons: pp. 26, 29, 46, 67, 85;
Producers, Inc.: p. 59.

Excerpts on pp. 34-35, 38 are from the 1984
presidential campaign debate presented by
The League of Women Voters Education Fund.

Excerpts on pp. 24-25, 50, 57-58 © Educational
Broadcasting Co. and GWETA.

Excerpts on pp. 44-47, 55-56, 62-63 copyright 1985 by
the Southern Educational Communications Association,
P.O. Box 5966, Columbia, S.C. 29250. Copies of the
complete transcript are available from SECA.

CONTENTS

ACKNOWLEDGMENTS

I am indebted to the following persons for their guidance and generous contributions of time and thought in providing source material as well as valuable insights into educational debating, both formal and informal:

Robert Branham, Ph.D., Director of Debate, Bates College, Lewiston, Maine, and Director of the Annual Summer Debate Institute for High School Debaters and Coaches at Bates College;

Wayne R. Cole, Chairman, History Department; and Garret M. Bensen, History and Social Studies Teacher, Lincoln Academy, Newcastle, Maine.

HOW TO DEBATE

THE PLEASURES AND BENEFITS OF DEBATING

1

If you've never taken part in a debate before, you'll be surprised and pleased at the benefits this experience can bring you, both personally and educationally. Whether it's an informal debate in the classroom, a speech competition, or a debating tournament, debating gives you the opportunity to develop poise and confidence in expressing your opinions and attitudes about any subject. You will also be developing skills in the use of language that will serve you well throughout your life.

Debating is not an activity you can approach casually. There's a certain amount of work and effort involved, but you will be well rewarded for whatever effort you put into it. You'll be learning how to think for yourself, and how to think on your feet in a fair-minded discussion. Whether you take the affirmative side (in favor) or the negative side (not in favor) of a controversial issue, you will be learning how to respect differences of opinion. Debating is free of the passion of a shouting match or personal argument. Instead, you will be concentrating on learning how to agree or disagree about a particular issue, based on your conception of the facts, evidence, and the good or evil of a situation or principle. There is also the enjoyment factor.

PERSONAL ENJOYMENT

As one debating teacher expressed it, "The first and most obvious benefit is personal enjoyment. A debater likes competitive debating. It's fun. Once you have taken part, once you have felt the thrill of matching wits with your opponents before an audience, no great sales effort is necessary to keep you interested."

Debating is a common experience in a country like the United States and other democracies, where everyone is free to express his or her opinion about anything under the sun. Every time there is an election, political candidates debate all the important issues trying to convince the public to vote for them.

There have been many famous debates in the history of our country. One of the most famous is the series of Lincoln–Douglas debates on the slavery issue. At that time, 1858, Abraham Lincoln was not well known. In fact, he was generally considered not much more than a competent, if colorless, small-town lawyer from Illinois. But when he began challenging the Democratic senator from Illinois, Stephen A. Douglas, he also began to make history.

MEMORABLE LANGUAGE

Debating can stimulate and inspire a person to use clear, concise, and memorable language. Americans have never forgotten some of the language Lincoln used in his debates with Douglas, such as the following: "A house divided against itself cannot stand. I believe

A painting depicting one of the famous Lincoln-Douglas debates.

this government cannot endure permanently, half slave and half free. It will become all one thing or all the other." Lincoln later became president and commander-in-chief of the Union forces in the Civil War of 1861–65, which led to the resolution of the slavery issue.

Scholars continue to study the Lincoln–Douglas debates not only because they provide such a rich and instructive storehouse of all the elements involved in debating, but also because the outcome was so important to the history of this country and its future development. You will find many examples in the chapters that follow, as well as some more recent examples of effective debating techniques.

One contemporary scholar, Harry V. Jaffa, professor of political philosophy at Claremont McKenna College, has focused on one of the most important elements in Lincoln's argument against his opponent. Professor Jaffa wrote in 1982: "Douglas's doctrine of 'popular sovereignty' meant no more than that: in a democracy justice is in the interest of the majority, which is 'the stronger.' "

A STANDARD OF RIGHT AND WRONG

According to Jaffa, "Lincoln, however, insisted that the case for popular government depended upon a standard of right and wrong independent of mere opinion and one which was not justified merely by the counting of heads. Hence the Lincolnian case for government of the people and by the people meant being for a moral purpose that informs the people's being." In other words, Douglas based his position on the rights or will of the majority, without considering the moral right or wrong of the proposition.

In one sense, this can be interpreted as the principle of "might makes right." Lincoln, on the other hand, was convinced of the moral right of those who opposed slavery. He stressed this theme repeatedly and in the end emerged victorious, not only in his debates with Douglas, but in the Civil War against the slave-holding states.

In the early part of this century, another famous debate concerned the issue of teaching Charles Darwin's theories of evolution. The debate centered on the 1925 trial of a high school teacher from Dayton, Tennessee, J.T. Scopes, who was accused of violating a state law that prohibited teaching evolution in public schools. Clarence Darrow, the famous trial lawyer, debated the case in defense of his client, Mr. Scopes. Although the initial verdict was against his client, Darrow is generally considered to have won the debate against his opponent, William Jennings Bryan, who debated for the prosecution. The conviction was later reversed by the Tennessee Supreme Court.

Darrow commented in his autobiography, "We entered the case solely to induce the public to stop, look, and listen, lest our public schools should be imperilled with a fanaticism founded on ignorance."

FAR FROM
SIMPLE ISSUES

These were complex issues for the people and leaders of the day. In fact, any question worthy of debate, as you will discover, is far from simple. It's easy to make a judgment based on ignorance, but once you get into the core of a problem or issue, simplicity vanishes.

You will also discover that one of the essentials involved in debating is thorough preparation. This means, among other things, that you must learn to examine a question critically, from both the affirmative and the negative sides. Whatever terms you use in your arguments to prove your case, for or against, must be defined with precision. You must also learn how to sift the relevant arguments from the irrelevant.

A typical scene during the Scopes "monkey" trial in 1925. William Jennings Bryan, who debated for the prosecution, is seated on the left; the defense attorney, Clarence Darrow, is standing with his arms folded.

Also, you will only have a certain amount of time to present a convincing argument or make an effective rebuttal. That makes it imperative that you use only the strongest and most relevant arguments you can devise. Nothing should be presented as part of your argument unless the reasoning and the evidence, in your opinion, are sufficient to prove your case.

INFORMAL VS. FORMAL DEBATING

In the chapters that follow, all of the discussions will be based on principles that apply to both informal and formal debating. The reason for this is that there are no set rules that apply only to informal educational debate. The only major differences between informal and formal debating are how the debates are organized, how strict the time limits may be, and how precisely the debate will be judged. The objective in both informal and formal debating is to be judged the winner, based on how thorough your preparation is, how convincing your arguments may be, and how skillful and effective is your delivery.

Whatever the judge's decision happens to be, whether your team wins or loses a debate, you will always come out a winner if you learn to respect the opinions of others. Along with developing your powers or reasoning and argument, that is one of the most important benefits of debating.

WHAT DEBATING IS AND HOW TO PREPARE FOR IT

2

The essence of debating involves taking sides on an issue and then presenting your arguments for or against that issue. For example, your instructor may ask your class to debate the following issue: "Peace in the World is More Important to Women Than to Men." In debating terms, this is called the *proposition.* In other words, the proposition defines the issue that will be debated. Your instructor may then ask for volunteers or select certain students to debate each side of the proposition, those for and those against.

There should be an equal number on each side or team. The number could be two, three, four or more, depending on the number specified by your instructor. Suppose there are four team members on each side. Those who are selected to argue in favor of the proposition are called the *affirmative team* members. Those who will be arguing against the proposition are called the *negative team* members.

THE NEXT STEP IS RESEARCH

Once you have been organized into affirmative and negative teams, the next step will be research. In this effort, you and your fellow team members will be searching through books, magazines, and other material that will help you find the *evidence* you need to present the strongest possible *arguments* to prove your *case.* A case consists of a set of reasons, arguments, supporting facts and other evidence presented in favor or against a proposition. You will be looking for facts, studies, and arguments that support your side of the proposition. You will also be looking for testimony of authority. This is the use of evidence, reports, and statements by agencies, organizations, and individuals whose authority, knowledge, and experience are widely known and respected.

In your research you will also become aware of some of the facts and arguments that the other side will probably be using to prove their case. This is valuable information that you and your fellow team members should include in your research notes. Later on you will find out why this information is valuable.

MEETING WITH TEAM MEMBERS

Before you begin your research, you and your team members will meet and discuss all the initial arguments that come to mind either in favor of or against the proposition, depending on which team you are on. This is one method of *analyzing the proposition* to find out the *main issues* involved. Each team member could then be assigned a particular source, a book or magazine article, for example, using the list provided by your instructor, from which to begin his or her research. A time limit of one or two weeks should be set for this phase of the research.

Using the books and other material your instructor has reserved in the school library for this purpose is a good beginning point. However, there may be many other sources at your disposal through school and local libraries, including other books, magazine articles, official documents, and transcripts of other debates on the issue.

When you have completed the initial research phase, your team will meet again and compare notes on the facts, arguments, and other evidence discovered. As you study this information, certain strong points will emerge. These strong points—your most convincing evidence and arguments—will represent and support your stand on the main issues to be debated in the proposition.

THE MAIN ISSUES

In discovering the main issues, keep in mind that it is not enough to concentrate only on your side of the issue or proposition. You must also be aware of all the opposing arguments. Notes should be taken on those as well. It is the only way in which you can discover all of the main issues in a proposition. If you neglect to do this, or are not as thorough in your analysis as you should be, one of the main issues you and your team members have overlooked may turn out to be a major point on which the case is won or lost.

THE IMPORTANCE OF EVIDENCE

For example, without studying your opponents' arguments, you may decide what you would like to prove. You may even discover the issues which you believe you can prove, based on the evidence you collect. You may feel confident that you have the advantage over your opponents. But you will not discover what you must prove in order to establish your case unless you know and understand what your opponents will be arguing.

Remember, too, that opinion counts for nothing. You can have an opinion about anything under the sun, but no one will take it seriously unless you can show that it is based on some kind of evidence. The same goes for any argument you may use in a debate. It "won't hold water," unless it is strongly supported by evidence.

The British biologist Thomas Huxley once said that scientists develop "a valuable habit of believing nothing unless there is evidence for it; and they have a way of looking upon belief which is not based on evidence not only as illogical but as immoral." The judge and audience (your classmates, for example) observing a debate may not be scientists, but they will be no less willing to accept any argument that is not based on evidence. In developing your skills as a debater, you will be acquiring the habit of neither offering nor accepting any statement as true unless it is based on evidence.

Here's a good example of using evidence to support an argument from a debate on "The Gender Gap," on the July 11, 1983, *MacNeil/Lehrer NewsHour* on public television. In defending her argument that there is a gender gap, that women do not have the economic advantages of men, Representative Olympia Snowe, Republican Congresswoman from Maine, declared:

The president received a mandate in 1980 to get the economy under control and we had to control inflation, and that certainly will have a ripple effect for all Americans. But nevertheless some of the budget programs were cut, and I think it disproportionately affected women. We were trying to realign programs, and the American people wanted that, and we can't go any further with respect to cuts in those particular programs. In fact, we have worked with the administration to insure that many of these programs would not be cut in the future or would not be recommended by the administration to be reduced. Women in this country are the last hired, the first fired. They feel the wrath of an ailing economy disproportionately, and therefore they're in a more precarious position. More women are single heads of households. More women who are heads of households live in poverty compared to men. I mean, the statistical data is there to show that women are in tenuous financial situations. So every policy that's implemented that affects women directly or indirectly, it affects them disproportionately so.

YOU CAN'T FORCE BELIEF

Another point to keep in mind is that you can't force belief. According to one historical account, Columbus and his crew swore that the island of Cuba was the mainland of what came to be known as the Western Hemisphere, even though this had not been proven. Anyone on his ship who dared to contradict him was told he would have his tongue slit.

We have long since learned that no one can be forced to believe in the truth of any argument unless it is based on fact, authority, or some other form of evidence. The same test that applies to the spoken word also applies to the printed word. The fact that a statement appears in print has nothing to do with its value as evidence unless it is based on fact or on the experience of a respected authority.

THE STRENGTH
OF THE EVIDENCE

Another important point to keep in mind is not to overestimate the strength of your evidence. The evidence

*Some debates simply confirm
the opinions we already hold.*

that you gather to prove your argument will tend to fall into three categories: Some may offer possible proof; some, probable proof; and some, actual proof. No matter how impressive it may be, however, all of your evidence taken together, in most cases, will seldom prove more than a high degree of probability. However, if it is strong enough, you have a good chance of winning the debate.

Once you and your team members have agreed on the main issues you will be arguing for or against in the debate, you will be selecting evidence to support your arguments. Taking notes based on research in a random manner will waste time and may cause confusion. Your research should be well-organized, and so should your system of note-taking.

TAKING NOTES

One method is to use either separate sheets of paper or 3 × 5 cards, writing only on one side. The notes on each sheet or card should refer to only one topic, either a main point or a subordinate point. Put the title of the topic at the top of the sheet or card.

Be selective in your note-taking. Note only those words which clearly and convincingly support your arguments. Quote directly from the source you are using and indicate this by putting quotation marks around the words quoted. Make sure your reference to the source is complete. It should include the name of the author, the title of the book or magazine article plus the name of the magazine, and the date of publication. Although only a small portion of the evidence you collect will actually be used during the debate, it gives you an important pool of information to draw from.

SELECTING EVIDENCE

Once the initial research is completed, you and your team members will meet again to discuss the results. if you agree that you now have all the evidence and arguments you need, the research could end there. However, you may also agree that more research is needed so you can build a stronger case. Another week may be allowed for this effort. This will depend on how much time your instructor has given you for research.

All of the information you gather will be used to serve two basic phases of a debate. One is the *opening statement* in which the person chosen by your team members will present your strongest arguments within the time limit allowed. This might be ten minutes. The other is for your *rebuttal.* The rebuttal is the response that the person chosen by your team members makes to your opponents' opening statement. Your opponents will also have the opportunity for a rebuttal.

Usually a shorter time is allowed for rebuttals than for opening statements. Each team might be allowed five minutes for its rebuttal. The team members chosen to make the opening statements and rebuttals will be expected to rehearse their presentations so they will be as clear and convincing as possible. (See Chapter 5 for some helpful suggestions.)

THE JUDGE'S DECISION

After the spokespersons for both sides have made their opening statements and rebuttals, the judge will decide which team has won the debate. The judge may be your instructor, or it could be another teacher, the headmaster or principal, or some other staff member of the school.

While each team is debating, the judge will be taking notes on the strength of the arguments presented and how well they are delivered. She or he may have a system of points by which the effectiveness of each team's opening statement and rebuttal is graded. This is the usual procedure in formal debating.

An informal debate may be structured in the following way:

SUGGESTED FORMAT
FOR INFORMAL DEBATE

The person chosen by the affirmative team makes her opening statement within the time limit agreed upon, which may be ten minutes, more or less.

The person chosen by the negative team makes his opening statement.

Time is then allowed for each team to prepare its rebuttal. This may be ten or fifteen minutes.

The person chosen by the affirmative team

You will be most successful in a debate if you take a strong position instead of watering down your arguments for fear of appearing extreme in your views.

makes her rebuttal speech within the time limit agreed upon, which may be five minutes, more or less.

The person chosen by the negative team makes his rebuttal speech.

The judge makes his or her decision as to which team has won the debate.

DON'T GET SIDETRACKED

Because of the time factor, and to increase your team's chances of winning the debate, you must be careful to keep to the main issues and not get sidetracked into less convincing facts and arguments. This applies to both your opening statement and your rebuttal. Never lose sight of that objective. You know that whatever arguments your side makes will be opposed, and you must be prepared to meet them head on, with even more convincing *counter-arguments* in your rebuttal.

A good example of finding the main issues can be found in a letter President Lincoln wrote to Major-General McClellan during the Civil War. Before he wrote the letter, Lincoln lined up all that could be said in favor of McClellan's plan against all that could be said in favor of his own plan.

Here is the letter:

Executive Mansion   February 3, 1862
Washington, D.C.

Major-General McClellan.

My dear sir:—You and I have distinct and different plans for a movement of the Army of the Potomac—yours to be down the Chesapeake, up the Rappahannock to Urbana, and across land to the terminus of the railroad on the York River; mine to move directly to a point on the railroad southwest of Manassas.

If you will give me satisfactory answers to the following questions, I shall gladly yield my plan to yours.

First. Does not your plan involve a greatly larger expenditure of time and money than mine?

Second. Wherein is a victory more certain by your plan than mine?

Third. Wherein is a victory more valuable by your plan than mine?

Fourth. In fact, would it not be less valuable in this, that it would break no great line of the enemy's communications, while mine would?

Fifth. In case of disaster, would not a retreat be more difficult by your plan than mine?

Yours truly,
ABRAHAM LINCOLN

One of the most respected authorities on the art and science of debating, William Trufant Foster, described finding the main issues in this way: "There is a main issue in all the affairs of life. Success depends on directing effort toward that issue. Without the ability to analyze a given situation and discover the particular difficulty to be overcome, i.e., the main issue, a man may waste his energy in blind endeavor, like a fly trying to escape through a window."

"HITTING THE NAIL ON THE HEAD"

According to Foster, the primary objective in discovering the main issues is to do so without getting sidetracked on unimportant or *subordinate issues.* He declared: "A thousand hard blows around a nail will not move it. One hard blow on the head will drive it in. The method of [finding] the main issue may be described as 'hitting the nail on the head.' "

Lincoln's letter to General McClellan is an example of a good beginning in discovering the main issues. He fully acknowledged opposing views, but countered with more convincing arguments that supported his views. Before he reached that point, however, we can assume that he spent a lot of time studying, thinking about, and discussing the problem.

METHODS
OF ARGUMENT

3

Whatever the proposition you will be debating, you will be using certain techniques of *logic* and *argumentation*, some consciously, some unconsciously. First, let's review the differences between logic and argumentation. According to one authority, the main purpose of logic is to make it possible for individuals and groups to distinguish between good and bad reasoning.

In argumentation, however, the main purpose is to convince and persuade people and urge them to action. Logic is concerned only with reason. Argumentation, on the other hand, is concerned not only with logical or convincing arguments but also with influencing belief or action through the appeal to emotion. Through argumentation, then, each team attempts to convince and persuade the judge and audience that its arguments in favor or against the proposition are stronger and therefore more convincing.

SOME BASIC METHODS
OF REASONING

Two common methods of reasoning used in debate are *inductive reasoning* and *deductive reasoning*. In inductive reasoning you start with specific facts or examples and thereby reach a generalization or conclusion. Here's an example of inductive reasoning.

There are nine known planets in the solar system: Mercury, Venus, Earth, Mars, Jupiter, Saturn, Uranus, Neptune, and Pluto. Each of these planets orbits around the sun. Therefore you can say as a generalization or conclusion that all the known planets in the solar system orbit around the sun.

Deductive reasoning works in the opposite way, moving from the general to the specific. Here's an example. Any person who is legally insane is considered incompetent to make a binding legal agreement. Joan Bill is legally insane. Therefore, Joan Bill is incompetent to make a binding legal agreement. Both of these examples are extremely simple, but they illustrate the basic structure of these types of reasoning.

Here are examples of inductive and deductive reasoning from the 1984 debate between the vice-presidential candidates, Congresswoman Geraldine Ferraro for the Democrats and Vice President George Bush for the Republicans. First an example of inductive reasoning, moving from a specific statement to a general conclusion, provided by candidate Ferraro. In discussing the war-and-peace issue, claiming that President Reagan's administration in its first term had not worked for peace, she declared:

Since today is Eleanor Roosevelt's* birthday, let me quote her. She said, "It's not enough to want peace;

---

*The wife of President Franklin Roosevelt, a Democrat, who served from 1932 to 1945.

you must believe in it. And it's not enough to believe in it; you must work for it." This administration's policies have indicated quite the opposite.

The last time I heard Vice President Bush blame the fact that they didn't meet with a Soviet leader—and this is the first president in forty years not to meet with a Soviet counterpart—he said the reason was because there (have been) three Soviet leaders in the past three-and-a-half years. I went and got a computer printout.

It's five pages of the leaders, world leaders, that the Soviet leaders have met with. And they are not little people. They are people like Mitterrand of France [François Mitterrand, president of France] and Kohl of Germany [Helmut Kohl, Federal Chancellor, Federal Republic of Germany], and President Kyprianou of Cyprus [Spyros Kyprianou, president of Cyprus]. And you go down the line—five pages of people that the Soviet leaders have managed to meet with—and, somehow, they couldn't meet with the president of the United States.

In addition to not meeting with his Soviet counterpart, this is the first president since the start of negotiating arms control agreements who has not negotiated an arms control agreement. But not only has he not negotiated one, he's been opposed to every single one that every other president has negotiated, including Eisenhower, including Ford, and including Nixon.

Over: Vice President George Bush and vice-presidential candidate Geraldine Ferraro during their 1984 television debate. Both were well spoken and forceful but perhaps a little too friendly with each other. Their hands seem to be expressing reasonableness, don't you think?

For an example of deductive reasoning, moving from a general statement to the specific, here's how candidate Bush responded to the argument that his running mate, President Reagan, had not made any progress in arms control or U.S.-Soviet relations.

We have made sound proposals on reducing nuclear weapons. The Strategic Arms Reduction Talks were good proposals. And it's the Soviets that left the table. The Intermediate Nuclear Force Talks were sound talks. And I wish the Soviet Union had continued them.

The chemical weapon treaty to ban all chemical weapons was our initiative, not the Soviets'. And we wish they would think anew and move forward to verification so that everybody would know whether the other side was keeping its word. But, much more important, you'd reduce the level of terror.

Similarly, we're talking to them in Vienna about conventional force reductions. We've talked to them about human rights. I've met with Mr. Andropov and Mr. Chernenko [Chernenko succeeded Soviet Premier Andropov when he died in office] to try to do something about the human rights question. This oppression of Soviet Jews is absolutely intolerable. And so we have to keep pushing forward on the moral grounds as well as on the arms reduction grounds.

But it is my view that because this president has been strong, and because we've redressed the imbalances, the Soviets are more likely to make a deal. The Soviets made an ABM (Antiballistic Missiles) treaty when they thought we were going to deploy an ABM system. So I am optimistic for the future, once they realize that we have this strong, principled president to negotiate with and yet demonstrate flexibility on arms control.

THE WEIGHT OF THE EVIDENCE

You will probably be using many methods of reasoning in presenting your case for or against a proposition. Other methods are explored in the next two chapters on affirmative and negative strategies during a debate. In argumentation, however, which is what debating is all about, the main concern is to show the likelihood that a given proposition is true or false.

The limits of time to research and debate a proposition, as well as the complexity of the proposition itself, in almost every case will make it impossible to prove that it is absolutely true or false under all circumstances.

Even though you may show great skill in using inductive and deductive reasoning and other methods to prove your arguments, you cannot expect to prove your arguments conclusively. Your goal must be to show that the *weight of the evidence*, in other words the strongest evidence and arguments, is on your side.

Your opponents will also be using inductive and deductive reasoning and other methods to prove their case. But if there are flaws in their arguments you should be alert to point them out in your rebuttal. Here's an example of how Lincoln exposed a major flaw in Douglas's reasoning:

The states must, without the interference of the General Government, do all those things that pertain exclusively to themselves—that are local in their nature, that have no connection with the General Government.

After Judge Douglas has established this proposition which nobody disputes or ever has disputed, he proceeds to assume, without proving it, that slavery is one of those little, unimportant, trivial matters, which are of just about as much consequence as the question would be to me whether my neighbor should raise horned cattle or plant tobacco; that there is no moral question about it, but that it is altogether a matter of dollars and cents.

That when a new territory is opened for settlement, the first man who goes into it may plant there a thing which, like the Canada thistle, or some other of those pests of the soil, cannot be dug out by the millions of men who will come thereafter; that it is one of those little things that is so trivial in its nature that it has no effect upon anybody save the few men who first plant upon the soil.

That it is not a thing which in any way affects the family of communities composing these states, nor any way endangers the General Government. Judge Douglas ignores altogether the very well-known fact that we have never had a serious menace to our political existence, except it sprang from this thing, which he chooses to regard as only upon a par with onions and potatoes.

CHALLENGES TO YOUR ARGUMENTS

Your opponents, in their efforts to prove their case and thereby disprove yours, will highlight all the important exceptions to whatever arguments you make and whatever conclusions you offer as evidence. These are the challenges that create excitement in a debate. They also put you on the defensive and make you work harder to prove your case.

One way in which to deflate some of the threatening evidence presented by your opponents is to admit all that you can safely admit, but no more. But be cautious. Admitting a point or argument that dangerously weakens your case can make the difference between winning or losing a debate. For these reasons, in preparing for a debate you must know and understand all the possible opposing arguments to your stand on the proposition and be well prepared to answer them.

When a minor point is made, one that you are certain cannot in any way damage your case, then it is safe to admit it. In doing this, you take some of the bite out of your opponents' charges. However, you must be prepared to counter with a strong argument.

This will make the minor point appear even less significant, and you will thereby strengthen your case. When charges are made that you cannot safely admit, it is even more important to counter with the strongest possible arguments that support your position.

TAKING THE AFFIRMATIVE SIDE

4

To be successful in affirmative debating you must accomplish three objectives:

1. You must be able to state clearly what must be done to establish the proof of a proposition.

2. You must accomplish this objective by means of convincing arguments.

3. Through reason *and* emotion, your arguments must be so convincing that you will persuade the judge and audience that you have proved the proposition.

YOUR OPENING STATEMENT

To accomplish these objectives you must concentrate on the main issues. These are the points on which the proofs of the proposition depend. In the first part of your opening statement, present the main issues clearly. Then state how you intend to prove these issues exist and that they support the affirmative's stand on the proposition.

In other words, you are saying to the judge and audience, "If I can prove these points, I can prove the proposition." You then proceed to argue your case, making it clear that you are doing what you said you would do to prove the proposition. At the close of your opening statement, summarize what you have done to prove your case and state that you believe you have done so convincingly.

Here's an example of the opening statement, made by James North, American author of the book *Freedom Rising: Life Under Apartheid Through the Eyes of An American on a Four-Year Clandestine Journey Through South Africa*, on "The Firing Line," April 1, 1985, a debate series on public television moderated by William F. Buckley, Jr.:

I would say that before I went to South Africa, partly through the works of Alan Paton and others, I had some sense that the system that prevailed there was quite similar to that in the American South up until fairly recently, up to the 1960s and certainly through the hundred years before that.

On arriving though, I could see that apartheid (the government system of racial segregation) is really a far more comprehensive system than that. In addition to segregated buses and beaches, what is known as petty apartheid, the kind of conditions that used to prevail in this country, there is a much more fundamental and widespread form of segregation. It's territorial segregation.

The country has been subdivided into 87 percent of the land area, which is for white ownership, and 13 percent of the country which is for black or African ownership. Blacks are only allowed into the white areas as so-called temporary sojourners. Many of them are migrant workers. Others live in the urban areas, perhaps 25 percent, but they have no permanent right to remain there and no right to own land or other property than personal property.

The centerpiece of the system is that the 70 percent of the country who are black are not South Africans. They do not have a permanent citizenship right in South Africa. They are directed to be citizens of these ten territories, the so-called Bantustans.

It's the equivalent of saying, "Let's abolish poverty in America. Let's take poor neighborhoods, let's say Harlem, certain counties in Appalachia, Watts in California, let's declare these areas separate countries. Let's take all poor people, people below a certain income, and declare them citizens of one of these areas, and then say we've abolished poverty in the United States."

CLAIMING MORE
THAN YOU CAN PROVE

In your conclusion to your opening statement, be careful not to claim more than you believe you have proved. If you claim more than you have actually proved, the judge and audience will probably react in one of two ways. Either they will think you are trying to deceive them in regard to the strength of your evidence, or that you have deceived yourself.

This may tend to make them view all of your evidence with suspicion. Don't exaggerate, don't argue that you have proved the proposition "beyond the shadow of a doubt." End with a strong conclusion, but don't assume that your evidence is beyond challenge. If it wasn't subject to controversy or argument, why would the proposition be debated?

A good example of what you might expect if you claim more than you can prove can be seen in the following response in the South African debate addressing Mr. North's claims that economic sanctions against

*Some debaters have a tendency
to talk a lot and say nothing.*

South Africa (denying South Africa economic support through investment and industry) would force the issue of racial equality. The response is from his opponent in the debate, John Chettle, a South African and director of the South Africa Foundation:

I think that people like Mr. North and people who want to make a genuine contribution to change in South Africa seem to always approach it from a punitive point of view: How can we punish those nasty racists and make them learn that they've got to shape up? And it seems to me that there are so many ways that in fact what is good in society can be recognized and pushed and helped, that in fact there should be more American investment because if anything it has been the biggest single overseas tool in breaking down separation.

I mean, after all, you cannot control a dynamic, evolving, economically prosperous society with a small coterie of white managers and skilled personnel. You just simply can't. And one of the things that has driven the government ultimately to recognize reality has simply been the fact that this economy has expanded, so opportunity for blacks has had to expand.

THE REBUTTAL SPEECH

In your rebuttal speech, your research and your understanding of both sides of the issue will provide you with the ammunition you need. So will careful attention to the arguments presented by your opponents in their opening statement. The time to prepare your rebuttal speech will be limited. In whatever time is allowed, be ready to sift through your note cards or sheets and select the evidence that will be most effective.

Also, as you listen to your opponents' opening statement, make notes, jotting down key words or phrases that will direct you to the evidence you need. This will include facts and statements from authorities that will deny or minimize your opponents' arguments and strengthen your position.

The rebuttal speech is an essential part of any debate. It gives both sides the opportunity to expand and reinforce their arguments. If a debate consisted only of an opening statement by each side, it would be the beginning but not the completion of what a debate is intended to be: a spirited clash of opinion. The affirmative side essentially presents a constructive case in favor of the proposition. That intention is maintained in the rebuttal speech.

However, the rebuttal speech is also destructive in the sense that its purpose is to destroy or deny the arguments of the negative side. As one debating authority expressed it: "Those who are to be convinced of the truth of a proposition wish to know not only why the arguments in favor are sound but also why the opposing arguments are unsound."

There are two basic ways in which you can attack your opponents' arguments. One deals with the facts or evidence presented, the other with the soundness of their reasoning. As to facts presented by your opponents, you can challenge the value and importance of those facts or show with evidence of your own that the facts supporting your case are stronger. As to the soundness of your opponents' reasoning, there are several types of unsound reasoning you can attack in your rebuttal speech. One is mistaking the cause for the effect.

A good example of this can be found in the debate between O'Connell of Ireland and Macaulay of England in Britain's House of Lords in 1833. O'Connell argued that the Act of Union, uniting Ireland with Great Britain, should be repealed, in other words, that Ireland should be allowed to govern its own country. The main issue he raised in favor of this argument concerned the disastrous conditions then existing in Ireland, for which he blamed the Union. In his rebuttal speech, Macaulay gave the following answer:

Ireland has undoubtedly just causes of complaint. We heard those causes recapitulated last night by the honorable and learned member, who tells us that he represents not Dublin alone, but Ireland, and that he stands between his country and civil war.

I do not deny that most of the grievances which he recounted exist, that they are serious, and that they ought to be remedied as far as it is in the power of legislation to remedy them. What I do deny is that they were caused by the Union, and that the Repeal of the Union would remove them. I listened attentively while the honorable and learned gentleman went through that long and melancholy list: and I am confident that he did not mention a single evil which was not a subject of bitter complaint while Ireland had a domestic parliament.

Is it fair, is it reasonable in the honorable gentleman to impute to the Union evils which, as he knows better than any other in the house, existed long before the Union? Post hoc: ergo, propter hoc [after this, therefore on account of it—an error in reasoning] is not always sound reasoning. But ante hoc: ergo, non propter hoc [before this, therefore not on account of it] is unanswerable.

The old rustic who told Sir Thomas More that Tenterden Steeple was the cause of Goodwin Sands reasoned much better than the honorable and learned gentleman. For it was not till after Tenterden Steeple was built that the frightful wrecks on the Goodwin Sands were heard of. But the honorable and learned gentleman would make Goodwin Sands the cause of Tenterden Steeple.

Some of the Irish grievances which he ascribes to the Union are not only older than the Union, but are not peculiarly Irish. They are common to England, Scotland, and Ireland; and it was in order to get rid of them that we, for the common benefit of England, Ireland, and Scotland, passed the Reform Bill last year.

A more contemporary example of how errors in reasoning can be attacked is found in "The Gender Gap" debate on the *MacNeil/Lehrer NewsHour,* referred to earlier. The speaker quoted is Kathy Teague, executive director of the American Legislative Exchange Council, a national organization of state legislators. Here's how she exposed an error in her opponent's reasoning that cutbacks in government programs had caused poverty among women:

Any federal grants or welfare programs that have been pared back under the Reagan Administration have not been what has resulted in poverty of women in America. The latest survey I saw showed that something like 50 percent of the American women believe that their greatest cause of poverty was divorce, and you certainly can't blame that on Ronald Reagan. The economic issues are the important issues, and Ronald Reagan has done what he promised the American people and American women that he would do. He has cut the inflation rate and he has cut our tax rate, and I think that's very important.

HOW THE
NEGATIVE ATTACKS

5

You must be thoroughly prepared in order to make a successful attack against the affirmative team's arguments. This means you must not only present effective arguments against the proposition but also know the strengths and weaknesses of the affirmative's side.

The same three steps that the affirmative side should take in preparing arguments in favor of the proposition should also be taken by the negative side. (1) You and your team members must be able to set forth clearly and concisely what must be done to overthrow the proposition. (2) You must do this by using convincing arguments. (3) You must be persuasive enough in your reasoning and in your emotional appeal to convince the judge and the audience that you have won the debate.

You must use the time allowed for your opening statement to present the main issues raised by the proposition. At the same time, you should tell the audience why you disagree with the affirmative side and how you intend to prove your case. The key to your team's success is preparation. Know all the probable and possible arguments the affirmative side may use and be prepared to counter with effective arguments of your own. If you are better prepared than the affirmative side, this could give you enough of an advantage to win the debate.

THE PROBABLE ARGUMENTS

That's why it's so important to study your opponents' probable arguments. You can only do this successfully by analyzing the proposition thoroughly enough to understand the main arguments on both sides of the question. Be careful not to sidestep or ignore important points in the argument, even though they do not help you prove your case. Senator Douglas made this mistake in his debates with Abraham Lincoln on the slavery issue. Here's an example of how Lincoln exposed Douglas:

It is precisely upon that part of the history of the country that one important omission is made by Judge Douglas. He selects parts of the history of the United States upon the subject of slavery, and treats it as the whole, omitting from his historical sketch the legislation of Congress in regard to the admission of Missouri, by which the Missouri Compromise was established, and slavery excluded from a country (the Missouri Territory) half as large as the present United States.

COMMENT: Here Lincoln accuses Douglas of ignoring the significance of the Missouri Compromise, an act of Congress in which the practice of slavery was forbidden in that territory. There is the added implication here that members of Congress, who are elected by the people, are duty-bound to reflect the will of the people in their districts on whatever question they vote. Therefore, this antislavery measure reflects the will of the people on this crucial question.

All this is left out of his history. And hence I ask how extraordinary a thing it is that a man who has occupied a position upon the floor of the Senate of the United States, who is now in his third term, and who looks to see the government of this whole country fall into his hands, pretending to give a truthful and accurate history of the slavery question in this country, should so entirely ignore the whole portion of that history—the most important of all.

COMMENT: Lincoln agains drives his point home, holding Douglas up to ridicule for pretending to speak on the entire slavery issue but ignoring this essential part of its history.

Is it not a most extraordinary spectacle, that a man should stand up and ask for any confidence in his statements, who sets out as he does with portions of history, calling upon the people to believe that it is a true and fair representation, when the leading part and controlling feature of the whole history is carefully suppressed?

COMMENT: This is Lincoln's way of saying that Douglas is being dishonest in his discussion of the slavery issue and therefore his judgment (and his arguments) should not be trusted. This is a good example of emphasizing an important point or argument through repetition.

SELECTING THE
STRONGEST EVIDENCE

In your research, you and your team members will be discovering a great deal of usable evidence to support your side of the proposition. It is good to find as much evidence as you can to make your arguments as strong as possible, but it can also be a problem unless you use it wisely. Using the first evidence that comes to hand is a poor approach and may weaken your argument. Keep collecting evidence within the time allowed for research, but once it has all been collected there are decisions to be made.

You and your team members must select only the strongest evidence that supports your case, and put the other evidence aside. One reason to hold onto it is that you might want to refer to some of it in your team's rebuttal if your opponents make reference to it in their opening statement.

Your approach in gathering evidence can be summed up in the words of one debating expert who said a debater should "read, read, read" and "think, think, think. And all the time he should be judiciously selecting, weighing, comparing, and rejecting." He also cautioned, "Let all the good pieces of evidence struggle for places in the argument: the law of selection must be the survival of the fittest."

Whatever evidence you decide to use, be careful not to overestimate its strength. No matter how strong your evidence may be, in all likelihood it will be conclusive only insofar as it demonstrates strong probability. For this reason, be careful not to claim more than the evidence justifies. If you exaggerate its worth, you will weaken your argument.

FINDING HOLES IN YOUR OPPONENTS' ARGUMENTS

One method of argument that your opponents may use is *argument from analogy.* When someone uses analogy, he or she infers that a certain fact known to be true of A is more likely to be true of B if B resembles A in certain essential characteristics or conditions. Lincoln was an acknowledged master of the use of analogy. For example, as the Civil War progressed some critics urged a change of commanders. Lincoln replied to this criticism by saying he thought it would be poor policy to change horses while crossing a stream.

When some people complained that the war was moving too slowly, this is how he responded:

> Gentlemen, I want you to suppose a case for a moment. Suppose that all the property you were worth was in gold, and you had put it in the hands of Blondin, the famous rope-walker, to carry across the Niagara Falls on a tight rope. Would you shake the rope while he was passing over it, or keep shouting to him, "Blondin, stoop a little more! Go a little faster!"
>
> No, I am sure you would not. You would hold your breath as well as your tongue, and keep your hand off until he was safely over. Now, the government is in the same situation. It is carrying an immense weight across a stormy ocean. Untold treasures are in its hands. It is doing the best it can. Don't badger it! Just keep still, and it will get you safely over.

Analogy must be used convincingly to be effective, otherwise it can fall on its face, be exposed as untrue or worthless. There's an example of this in the debate between Chettle and North over South Africa's political policies. First, the analogy put forth by Mr. North:

What we have there (in South Africa) is a situation analogous to Nazi Germany in the 1930s. I use the word analogous in that meaning. It's not identical. There are certainly various features that are different between the two regimes. But I see South Africa in all of the events of the last six months or the last few years drifting towards increased war, increased internal violence, and this little-known war in Namibia I talked about, and I see that there has to be something done to try and bring some end to this.

Here's how Mr. Chettle exposed the weaknesses in Mr. North's analogy:

The trouble is that whenever we do anything good it's apparently because we want to keep our international image right, and whenever we do anything bad we're really showing our natural colors. I actually resent this analogy, which Bishop Tutu uses too, with Nazi Germany. In Nazi Germany, were there any opposition parties? Were there human rights groups organized and recognized and articulate? Was there a free press and an outspoken press? Was there an independent judiciary? The whole thing is laughable. There are things that one hates and dislikes and wants to get changed in South Africa, but to use this analogy simply makes the thing ludicrous.

When your opponents use one or more analogies in their arguments, you may be able to quash them by proving one of the following:

1. The details of comparison and contrast are not essential to the question at issue.
2. The points of difference outweigh the points of likeness.
3. The conclusion reached by the analogy can be discredited by other kinds of proof.
4. The fact known to be true of the analogous case is less likely to be true of the case in question.
5. The alleged facts on which the analogy is based are false.

EXPOSING ERRORS
IN REASONING

A good debater on the negative side will always be on the alert for *errors in reasoning*, ready to expose them both in the opening statement and in the rebuttal. When you have made a thorough preparation for a debate, you know what arguments will probably be used by the affirmative side. Knowing this, you can anticipate what arguments your opponents will try to stress. As you listen to your opponents' opening statement you can quickly make notes on what arguments are used and be prepared to answer them by pointing out errors in reasoning.

Errors in reasoning are known as *fallacies.* There are two basic types of fallacy. One type of fallacy results from reasoning that is unclear in proving what caused certain conditions to exist. Another type of fallacy can result from reasoning that fails to prove that certain conditions will have a particular result.

You can expose fallacies by (1) proving that something else caused the conditions to exist, or (2) proving that the causes named by your opponents could not have produced or are not solely responsible for a particular situation. With either method you accomplish an important objective by casting doubt on the soundness of your opponents' arguments.

Here's how Ann Lewis, a member of the Democratic National Committee, responded to an argument that President Reagan had made more appointments of women than Democrats in the past, during the debate on "The Gender Gap":

There are lots of ways to do those statistics, without pulling them all out and putting everybody to sleep. If you look, for example, at appointments requiring Senate confirmation, which is an awfully good way to see

*which are policymaking positions and which are not,
Ronald Reagan's appointments are far below those of
the last Democratic administration. If you look at the
appointment of women as judges, which is a critical
issue when we think of how much of our lives are
decided by the courts, and how much especially
because we are not yet in the Constitution (a reference
to the Equal Rights Amendment), how much we have to
depend in daily life on the courts, Ronald Reagan's
record of appointing women as judges is just shame-
ful.*

An example of how it can be disproved that an alleged
cause produced a certain effect can be seen in a hypothetical murder trial. The prosecuting attorney tries to
prove that the defendant committed the murder, but
unless she has the facts to prove it, the defendant, even
though she is guilty, may go free.

In the absence of conclusive evidence, the defense
attorney, on the other hand, tries to prove that her client
either had no motive to commit the murder, or, if she
did, that she did not have sufficient opportunity. She
may also be able to prove that someone else had an
even stronger motive.

SHOWING THE ABSURDITY OF
YOUR OPPONENTS' ARGUMENT

Some of your opponents' arguments may appear to be
so ridiculous, so poorly reasoned, that you will be able
to use the *reductio ad absurdum* technique. Reductio
ad absurdum is a Latin expression which means "to
reduce to absurdity." This is a technique in which an
argument is disproved by showing the absurdity of its
conclusion.

Here are two examples. A lawyer, perhaps in a
moment of spite, once asserted in court that a corpora-

Former Senator George McGovern (left) debating columnist William F. Buckley (right) on one of Buckley's "Firing Line" shows, taped at Yale University in 1978. Buckley is well known for the way he uses language and for his attacking debate style.

tion could not make an oral contract because a corporation has no tongue. The judge was quick to reduce this argument to absurdity by declaring, "Then, according to your own argument, a corporation could not make a written contract because it has no hand."

A more serious example relates to the controversy over slavery in the eighteenth and nineteenth centuries. Some people were opposed to the idea of freedom for black slaves and other subjugated people because the slave and the subjugated were unprepared to accept the responsibilities of freedom. Edmund Burke, the eighteenth-century British statesman and philosopher, and one of the most intelligent politicians of the day, had this answer:

Many politicians of our time are in the habit of laying it down as a self-evident proposition, that no people ought to be free till they are fit to use their freedom. The maxim is worthy of the fool in the old story, who resolved not to go into the water until he had learned how to swim. If men are to wait for liberty until they become wise and good in slavery, they may indeed wait forever.

THE NEGATIVE REBUTTAL

Some of the basic tools that can be used to good effect in a rebuttal speech have been discussed in the previous chapter from the affirmative's point of view. They can work just as well for the negative side in its efforts to overcome the affirmative's arguments. Two basic fundamentals that apply, no matter which side you are on, are perceptive thinking and reasoning, and a thorough knowlege of both sides of the question. You must use these basic tools to good effect in both your opening statement and in your rebuttal. They are particularly important in making your rebuttal effective. Keep in mind that your rebuttal is your last opportunity in which to convince both the judge and the audience that your side has the stronger and more convincing arguments.

The notes you take when the affirmative side makes its opening statement and then its rebuttal speech should be your guide. Be on the lookout for flaws in the affirmative's arguments. Be ready to challenge any opinions expressed that are not based on reliable facts. Also be on the lookout for any *inconsistencies* in their arguments. In his debates with Douglas, Lincoln was able to challenge his arguments on more than one occasion by exposing inconsistencies, as in the following example.

During his debates with Lincoln in 1859, Senator Douglas maintained that the people of a territory had the lawful right to exclude slavery from its limits, in spite of the Dred Scott Decision of the U.S. Supreme Court. Lincoln exposed the inconsistency of Douglas's argument by declaring:

The Dred Scott Decision expressly gives every citizen of the United States a right to carry his slaves into the United States Territories. And now there was some inconsistency in saying that the decision was right, and saying, too, that the people of the Territory could lawfully drive slavery out again. When all the trash, the words, the collateral matter, was cleared away from it—all the chaff was fanned out of it—it was a bare absurdity: no less than that a thing may be lawfully driven away from where it has a lawful right to be.

Here again is where your perceptive thinking and reasoning will come into play. If you realize that some of your arguments lack the strength to be convincing, do not pursue them in your rebuttal. Where your arguments are strongest, however, reemphasize them as strongly as possible. Emphasis can be a very effective debating tool. In this final thrust, you should expose the weakness of the affirmative's arguments as tellingly as possible, and at the same time, pursue your most convincing lines of attack.

A good example of emphasizing the strong arguments on one side of a proposition and attempting to expose an opponent's weaknesses can be seen in this exchange of rebuttals between North and Chettle on the South African question.

Mr. North: *On the argument that economic growth will lead to expanding economic opportunities for the blacks, to some extent it has. But (I disagree) that this would in turn translate into an erosion of apartheid, that the police state would start to dissolve, that the Bantustan system, the blacks' inability to have property rights in urban areas, these various forms of things would change, you know, phenomenally, due to this.*

Now during the 1960s South Africa had one of the highest rates of economic growth in the world and again in 1980 and '81 there was an enormous boom in the country. Gold prices were fairly high and the economy, I think, went up eight percent in 1980 and five percent the next year, and none of this was translated into any serious reform within the country.

Mr. Chettle: *But that's not true. I mean, you get, for example, for the first time in 300 years, coloreds* and Indians—not yet blacks, but coloreds and Indians—in the South African parliament. You have a colored and an Indian actually in the South African cabinet participating in the legislation which governs the country. For the last 18 months there have been conversations and discussions with major black leaders as to how blacks can be brought into the process.*

It is going to be extraordinarily difficult. I mean, how we are actually going to solve this problem, I often wonder myself. But to think that somehow the only way that you can get people to deal with it is by beating them

---

*Persons of mixed racial background, e.g., those who have both white and black ancestors.

over the head with a two-by-four seems to me to be the actual reverse of the truth.

Even a country like New Zealand, which is one of the least recalcitrant of nations as far as I've been able to see, is getting very irritated with the United States beating it over the head because of the anti-nuclear stance that they've taken. Now, I happen to think that that anti-nuclear stance that they've taken is silly. But my point is that this rouses the nationalism and the resistance of people. They don't like being told by other people how they should conduct their affairs. And Americans no more like it than South Africans do.

LISTENING TO YOUR OPPONENT, RESPONDING EFFECTIVELY

6

No matter how strong your opening statement may be, be prepared to answer your opponents' arguments in your rebuttal speech. To do that successfully, listen carefully to all the opposing arguments and be fully prepared to answer them, especially those that question your credibility and thereby threaten your position on the proposition. You must make a strong response, a response that is convincing and persuasive, in order to be judged the winner.

As always, the key is preparation, being aware of all the main points on both sides of the issue and having the strongest possible evidence to support your views. You can probably anticipate most of the arguments your opponents may use, but be prepared for surprises.

Through research, you'll know your own strong and weak points, and you will also discover and make note of your opponents' strong and weak arguments. But you must respond to what you read and make it your own. This will happen when you select the evidence and arguments you will be using. It will also happen when you and your team members prepare in advance for your rebuttal speech.

A skillful debater may have enough rebuttal material to talk for an hour, even though she or he knows there may be only five minutes allowed. The great advantage, however, is that you lessen the chances of being surprised by your opponents' line of attack and have the material you need to respond effectively. A skillful debater will also carefully group his or her evidence and material in anticipation of what the opponents' main lines of attack may be.

AN UNSUSPECTED ARGUMENT

But what if you are surprised by an unsuspected argument or unfamiliar evidence? You won't have time to collect new evidence for your rebuttal. The only alternative left is to decide as quickly as you can just what bearing it has on the proposition and what its relation is to your own arguments. You will also have to use your judgment in deciding whether it's worth answering. If it is, then you will have to find evidence and arguments strong enough to rebut it successfully.

A slipshod approach to your opponents' rebuttal can only be disastrous. If you know the main issues, the major arguments on both sides of the question, there is no need to jot down a lot of miscellaneous points made by your opponents that are not worth answering. Some of your opponents' points may be concerned with minor issues, not the main issues, and therefore not worth arguing. Don't waste time and thought on these. Stick to the main issues and drive your own points home.

If you are well prepared, you have already laid the groundwork for an effective rebuttal. You will have your

*Sometimes more than one
debater's arguments are stupid.*

evidence sheets or 3 × 5 cards, each headed by a separate topic describing the evidence or argument. It may also be helpful to number each card or sheet consecutively and then make a numbered list of topics for quick reference. This will save time. The time allowed for you and your team members to prepare for your rebuttal will be limited. It might be ten or fifteen minutes, and you should be prepared to work as quickly as you can.

GETTING OFF THE TRACK

There may be times when some of the statements made by your opponents are so illogical, or so far from the point, that they appear stupid and pointless. It may be tempting to come up with a statement in your rebuttal that will embarrass your opponents by holding them up to ridicule, but don't do it. That can get you off the track, and is known as *introducing personalities* into a debate.

Calling your opponents "stupid," for example, won't win you any points with the judge or the audience. Point out the errors that have been made by your opponents, but don't dwell on them. Stick to the main line of your argument and drive your own points home.

UNITY AND EMPHASIS

Your best attack, both in your opening statement and in your rebuttal, is a *unified attack*. What this means is that all of your arguments and evidence should fit together as a whole. Introducing personalities is not the only way you can get off the track, and destroy a unified approach.

You can do this by relying too heavily on statements of authority, anecdotes, and personal comments. If you have prepared your opening statement well, all of your evidence and arguments will fit together. They have one unified purpose: to reinforce your stand on the proposition.

Use the same approach in your rebuttal, making the best possible use of the time allowed. Here is where you can make skillful use of emphasis by repeating your strongest arguments. It may not hurt your case if the judge and audience forget some of your less important points, the subordinate issues, but stress your major arguments. Emphasize them through skillful repetition so they will not be forgotten.

In his debates with Lincoln, Douglas asserted again and again "the right of the people of a state to settle the question of slavery for themselves," and demanded "obedience to the decision of the highest tribunal in the land, the Supreme Court." Similarly, Lincoln turned again and again to his main argument that "a house divided against itself cannot stand; this government cannot endure permanently half-slave and half-free."

Also, Lincoln reminded his audiences again and again that Douglas had said, "I do not care whether slavery is voted up or down." When you are repeating your main arguments, try to express them in phrases so clear, exact, and striking that they will bear frequent repetition.

USING A FLOWSHEET

One valuable tool you may want to use in taking notes while your opponents are speaking is a *flowsheet*. A flowsheet accomplishes two important objectives: (1) it will save time by helping you to organize your notes and comments for use in your team's rebuttal; (2) it will help make your notes as complete as possible because they will be grouped under specific arguments. A legal-size note pad is recommended for use as a flowsheet. It should be headed by the following four columns:

Affirmative Case	Negative Case	Affirmative Counter Argument	Negative Counter Argument

If you are on the affirmative side, in Column 1 outline your team's case as it will be presented in your opening statement, but in abbreviated form. Use short phrases, sometimes only a few words or even one word, as long as it provides enough of an indication of the argument or evidence.

Use the same approach in Column 2, where you indicate the main points and evidence on the negative side presented by the negative team in its opening statement. This, of course, must be done quickly, as you listen to the negative's opening statement. Here

FLOWSHEET FOR PROPOSITION: "Peace in the world is more important to women than to men."

Affirmative Case	Negative Case	Affirmative Counter Arguments	Negative Counter Arguments
women for peace history Europe US	men leaders—peace efforts	men—waged war, broken peace	both men and women involved in war decisions
women leaders—peace movements antinuke UN	Lincoln—Civil War	Lincoln's uncond. surrender	psych. studies—women equally agressive
recent studies Carnegie Foundn. Brookings Inst.	Pres. Wilson—League of Nations	Soviet–US relations	women—involved in war decisions—US, Europe
psychological studies Princeton Amer. Psych. Assn.	UN—founded by men	UN not working	no one works harder than men for peace—record speaks for itself
women should have more active roles	other peace movements led by men	women in forefront of peace organizations	
	physicians for peace, other groups		
	male leaders		

again, a thorough knowledge of the negative side of the issue as well as your own, reinforced with notes on sheets or 3×5 cards, will prove valuable.

In Column 3, list the arguments and evidence your team will be using in your rebuttal. If you have numbered or coded your 3×5 cards or sheets, you can just use the number or code, another time saver. Otherwise, use short phrases to indicate this. Use Column 4 to indicate the counter arguments used by the negative side in its rebuttal.

Use the flowsheet in the same way if you are on the negative side. Whichever team you are on, you will be under a certain amount of pressure to get as much information down as possible, in a limited amount of time.

It will also help if you are able to develop some kind of *shorthand*, so you can get down as much information as you think you will need for an intelligent response. When you take notes in class you probably use some version of shorthand for the same reason. Some words are not written at all because you know where to fill them in. This would probably be true of certain articles, adjectives, conjunctions, and helping verbs.

If you don't have a shorthand system, ask your instructor for directions in developing a system you can use to good effect during a debate. Whatever system you develop, make sure your notes are legible and accurate. On page 70 is an example of how a flowsheet might be used if you were debating the proposition: "Peace in the World Is More Important to Women Than to Men."

MAKING YOUR DELIVERY EFFECTIVE

7

The preferred method of delivery in debating and other forms of public speaking is to speak extemporaneously, that is, without notes. However, this is an art that requires several years and wide experience for most people to master. As a beginning debater you should concentrate on another alternative: skillful speaking from organized notes. This, too, is an art, if it is to be done well.

One method you may want to use in learning this art is to write out your opening statement in its entirety, making sure you have covered all the main points. Then condense this material down to an outline, using complete sentences for the main points and partial sentences or phrases for the evidence that supports them. Then practice speaking from your outline, filling in where complete sentences are needed. Take care that your speech has continuity, without any long pauses in delivery. The more you practice, the less likely there will be any long, noticeable pauses. With practice, it will begin to sound fluent and polished, just the way you want it to sound when you make your opening statement during the debate.

A SAMPLE OUTLINE

Suppose you have been chosen by your team to make the opening statement on the hypothetical proposition: "Peace in the World Is More Important to Women Than to Men." Here's a sample outline for that proposition from the affirmative team's point of view.

OUTLINE FOR OPENING STATEMENT
BY AFFIRMATIVE TEAM MEMBER ON
THE PROPOSITION:
"PEACE IN THE WORLD IS MORE
IMPORTANT TO WOMEN THAN TO MEN."

I. Women have worked for peace throughout history
   A. Examples from European history
   B. Examples from American history

II. No group is working harder today to achieve peace in the world than groups led by women
   A. Examples of women leaders of peace movements, such as the Antinuclear Freeze
   B. Women leaders in the United Nations who work for peace

III. Studies prove that women are much more inclined to seek peaceful solutions to political problems and military crises than men
   A. Examples of recent studies (e.g., from organizations such as the Carnegie Foundation, the Brookings Institution and others)
   B. Psychological studies that show women are more interested in peace than men

IV. Summing Up: If we are to achieve peace in the world, then women must play more active roles because they are the peace-seekers

IMPROVING YOUR VOICE

When you are debating, a great deal of the audience's attention will be focused on your voice. Be sure of the pronounciation of words and use a variety of tones so your voice won't sound monotonous. Also, be sure to emphasize the main points of your arguments, using good vocal techniques. These and other qualities you bring to your presentation can help or hinder the persuasiveness of your arguments. Spending enough time rehearsing your opening statement will help; so will the use of a tape recorder so you can hear exactly how you sound.

Students who sing in a chorus or church choir have one advantage in that they have learned how to control their breathing. This helps them make long statements without pausing for breath. Even if you are not a singer, however, you can also develop a good speaking voice by using vocal exercises and techniques recommended for speakers.

For example, practice expelling the air from your lungs in short, sharp gasps. As you do this, place your hand on your abdomen so you can feel the tightening or inward contraction of your stomach muscles as air is expelled from your lungs. Then try using sounds as air is expelled. Say Hep! Hep! Hep! or bah, bay, bee, bi, bo, boo or some other combination of sounds.

ANOTHER BREATHING EXERCISE

Another exercise to improve control of breathing is to fill your lungs with air and then exhale as slowly as possible. Time yourself to see how long you can keep exhaling without stopping. Keep in mind that the object is not to get as much air as you can into your lungs but how slowly you can let the air out.

Then try vocalizing again. As you slowly let the air out of your lungs, utter a long, continuous hum. Then try an "oo" sound and other vowel sounds. Don't let the sound become "breathy." Keep the tone clear. One way to make sure the air is being let out of your lungs as slowly as possible is to hold a lit candle close to your mouth. The flame should flicker but not go out.

IMPROVING TONE QUALITY

Using the words in the list below, intone each word quietly at first and then louder and louder. Try to give the tone a ringing quality by letting the word vibrate in your throat. Avoid breathiness by not using too much air. As you intone the words, put your fingertips on your nose and cheekbones to see if you can feel a vibration.

one	home	drone	alone	phone
rain	plain	nine	lean	spoon
ring	nine	gong	moon	fine

MAKING YOUR WORDS DISTINCT

Another good exercise for improving voice quality as well as pronunciation is to read aloud a favorite passage from prose or poetry, or a lyric from a favorite song. Do this slowly at first, making sure all of the words are pronounced correctly, and then faster until you've reached a normal rate of speaking.

You can improve the clarity of your speaking voice by paying special attention to the distinctness of the words. Practice saying tongue-twisters as clearly and rapidly as you can, such as the following:

She sells sea shells by the sea shore.
National Shropshire Sheep Association.
Are you copper-bottoming them, my man?
No, I'm aluminuming 'em, mum.
He sawed six long, slim, sleek, slender saplings.
Dick twirled the stick athwart the path.
Rubber baby-buggy bumpers.
Sarah, Sarah, sitting in a shoe shine shop.

VOWELS AND CONSONANTS

Improving the distinctness of your speech through careful enunciation of vowels and consonants will lend persuasiveness to your opening statement and rebuttal. As one debating expert cautioned: "Many people swallow their vowels and ignore their consonants. Especially flagrant is this fault at the end of sentences, which as a rule should deserve the greatest emphasis. Earnest, sustained practice in enunciation is necessary. It may be exaggerated in practice with no danger of exaggeration in public." All of the words you speak in a debate are important. It is your responsibility to make sure they are heard, and given the emphasis they deserve.

WHEN YOU GET UP TO SPEAK

You probably won't be able to avoid a certain amount of nervousness and tension when you get up to speak. This is natural, and to a certain degree it is good for you because it tends to heighten your awareness and your desire to perform well. However, do whatever you can to control this nervousness and not let it detract from your delivery. How you stand and act during your delivery is important.

Try to look ready and relaxed. Avoid any eccentricities that will be distracting, such as slouching, long pauses, speaking too slowly or too quickly. Stand erect, speak straightforwardly, and be as composed as you can.

Avoid flamboyant gestures to emphasize major points. As a general rule, deliberate gestures are not necessary in debating. Whatever gestures come as you speak, such as raising your arms, pointing a finger, making a fist, making a sweeping motion with your hand, for example, should come naturally. Do not make conscious gestures.

If you are well prepared and interested in your subject, there will be a certain amount of body movement and gesturing, but it will never be exaggerated, and will therefore not distract from your delivery.

Speak as naturally as possible, with no pretense, no staginess that will turn off the audience. If you tend to overdo certain gestures, even though they may come naturally, your instructor will point this out to you.

READING QUOTATIONS

Rather than commit all of the evidence to memory or depend on an outline and notes, occasionally you may want to read a quotation directly from the source, such as a book, magazine, or official government report. This can be very effective. However, you must practice reading the quotation aloud so you can make your point as effectively as possible.

You don't want to stumble in the reading, giving the audience the impression that you really aren't familiar with the material. Also, continue to make eye contact with the audience while reading, never taking your eyes off them for more than a second or two.

Note the words you want to emphasize and have the section you want to read well marked so you can find it quickly. Time is of the essence in both the opening statement and the rebuttal. Reading the exact words from one of your most important sources of evidence will tend to increase its credibility. However, don't do this so often that it becomes distracting and monotonous.

PRACTICING YOUR DELIVERY

Once you have written your opening statement in full and then condensed it into an outline, the next step is to practice your delivery. This will be difficult to do smoothly until you have practiced many times. As you go through this step in preparation, the important thing is not to get discouraged. Even though there may be occasional pauses at first, keep going over the material until your delivery is as smooth as you can make it.

Time yourself to see how many of the main points you can include in your opening statement within the time that will be allowed. When you begin to feel confident about your delivery, practice in front of a friend or family member and ask them to be critical. This will help you improve your delivery and eliminate any eccentricities or gestures that are inappropriate or distracting.

Ask the person listening to you the kinds of questions that will be helpful, such as: Is the language clear? Is the argument convincing? Am I emphasizing the right words? Make your style of delivery conversational. Speak as if you were talking to a small group of friends or classmates. Don't be stiff and "oratorical."

Make your transitions as smooth as possible as you move from point to point. There are many ways in which you can indicate this. For example, change the rate of delivery, the tone, the volume, or your position as you address the audience. Other methods include changing the emphasis, using a gesture that comes naturally, and skillfully using pauses.

*Two presidential hopefuls during their fourth
televised debate preceding the 1960 presidential
election: Senator John F. Kennedy gestures as
Vice President Richard M. Nixon awaits his turn.
Kennedy, who went on to win the election, was
justly admired for his oratorial prowess.*

HOW TO USE EMPHASIS

You'll know which are the strongest points in your argument, but to highlight their importance you must give them sufficient emphasis. The judge and audience won't be sifting through your arguments to find out which are the strongest. You will have to indicate this and make those arguments memorable.

One recommended technique is to utter the words in a major argument with concentrated deliberation. Stop abruptly and pause in the right places. Use a natural gesture to attract attention. Lower your tone and slow the rate of delivery, or increase the volume and the pace. Anything you can do to increase the attention of judge and audience to your main points will help you give them the emphasis they deserve.

A PERSUASIVE AND CONVINCING DELIVERY

Through good delivery techniques, do whatever you can to make your opening statment and your rebuttal persuasive and convincing. One way to do this is to put your full concentration on what you are saying. What you say and how you say it—the message—should be your chief concern. For this reason, a simple, direct approach is the best technique. Don't beat around the bush. Come right to the point and stay with it throughout your delivery.

In your rebuttal you can show you are fair-minded by admitting some points that are safe to admit. Give your opponents their due, as long as your arguments are not damaged. Never avoid an important issue raised by your opponents. Fairness in itself can be persuasive because it demonstrates to the judge and audience that you understand both sides of the question. Try to maintain good self-control and don't let your emotions get the upper hand.

This is particularly important in your rebuttal speech, in which you are responding directly to your opponents. Answer their arguments clearly and firmly, and restate your own arguments as strongly as possible.

If you can think of a humorous situation, story, or analogy that exposes a weakness in your opponents' arguments, you may want to consider injecting some humor into your presentation. This can be effective as long as the humor is appropriate. However, the humor should be brief and not take precious time away from the main thrust of your arguments.

When you are using humor to drive home a point or to expose your opponent's errors in reasoning, make sure the audience is laughing with you and not at you. Nothing is more wasted or pointless than humor that has nothing to do with the arguments involved in debating a proposition.

A PERSUASIVE SPEAKER

In learning how to be a persuasive speaker you will realize that people are willing to be led if they are convinced your arguments are reasonable, but you can't force them to think as you do, or to accept your opinions and arguments. You must persuade them. In doing this, you must also appeal to their emotions.

But persuasion will not be possible unless you speak with conviction and convince the judge and audience that your side has the stronger arguments. Use all the recommended speaking techniques you can master in reaching this objective. However, remember that conviction is a matter of reason, and reason is based on logic. Your arguments must be logical, and your evidence must be convincing.

HOW JUDGES MAKE
THEIR DECISIONS

8

Whether it's an informal or formal debate, judging is a difficult task. Certain basic elements will be considered before a decision is reached, including the following:

1. The strengths and weaknesses of the arguments
2. How well the challenged arguments are answered
3. The errors in evidence and reasoning that are pointed out or ignored by either team
4. The effectiveness of the delivery

The most important question that a debating judge must decide, of course, is which team was more effective in debating the proposition. He or she will be taking notes throughout the debate, gathering evidence to justify his or her decision.

A good debating judge will be familiar with all the elements involved in debating. There may be times when the judge is especially knowledgeable about the proposition being debated, but this knowledge must be put aside and not influence the decision. The judge must consider only the evidence and reasoning that both sides introduce during a debate. Even though some of the evidence presented may be superficial or incomplete (based on the judge's knowledge of the subject), the participants should be judged on *their* knowledge, not the judge's.

When weak evidence is presented it must be accepted by the judge at its face value within the context of the debate. However, the strengths and weaknesses of the arguments and evidence presented by both sides will be evaluated. If the judge uses a *ballot*, he or she will indicate this by the use of quality-rating points or some other system of evaluation. This must be done carefully and fairly. When it is obvious that one team could have taken a much stronger position on a particular issue, the judge must also note whether the opposing team countered or challenged that particular argument.

Every debate must be judged within its own framework. For this reason, almost any statement made or position taken by either the affirmative or negative side will stand until denied by an opposing argument or evidence. Any errors of omission or failure to challenge an argument or evidence will be so noted. If the debate is informal, the judging may also tend to be informal. But it will serve its purpose as long as the basic elements in judging are covered.

THE CASE SUMMARY METHOD

In judging formal debates, however, certain methods will be used. For example, one is the *Case Summary Method.* In this method the judge records an outline of

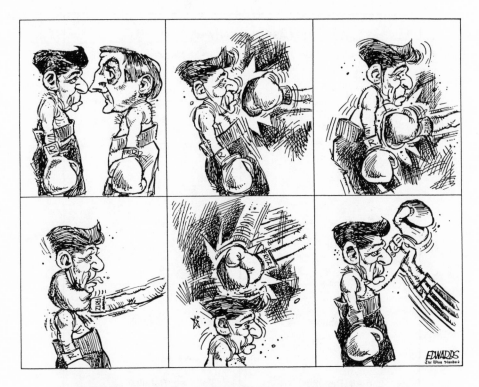

President Reagan and former Vice President Walter F. Mondale squared off in televised debates during the 1984 presidential campaign. Despite the message implied by the cartoon, most people win debates on the basis of their debating skills.

the case. Using a sheet of paper with a line dividing it in half vertically, the judge records the issues and evidence presented by the affirmative on one side and the negative on the other. Several sheets of paper may be needed. An example of a sheet used in the Case Summary Method is shown on page 86.

THE CASE SUMMARY METHOD

Affirmative	Negative

1st Aff.

I. _____

    A. _____

    B. _____

II. _____

    A. _____

    B. _____

. . . etc.

2nd Aff.

I. _____

. . . etc.

1st Aff. Rebuttal

I. _____

. . . etc.

2nd Aff. Rebuttal

I. _____

. . . etc.

1st Neg.

I. _____

    A. _____

    B. _____

    C. _____

II. _____

    A. _____

        1. _____

. . . etc.

2nd Neg.

I. _____

. . . etc.

1st Neg. Rebuttal

I. _____

. . . etc.

2nd Neg. Rebuttal

I. _____

. . . etc.

From *Argumentation and Debate*, by Austin J. Freeley, © 1961 by Wadsworth Publishing. Reprinted with permission.

Each judge will have his or her own style in making use of this sheet. Some will use different colored pencils or draw lines from one item to another. Some judges have their own symbols to indicate how the arguments develop, where the opposing arguments clash, and to record other information. This may include notes on the effectiveness of delivery.

THE ISSUE SUMMARY METHOD

Another method used by some judges in formal debates is the *Issue Summary Method.* This also involves sheets of paper, but in this method horizontal lines are used. Each issue is assigned a horizontal column, with Roman numerals used to identify each issue. As each issue is developed or challenged by affirmative or negative speakers, the judge indicates this by using a triple X (XXX).

The arguments of the first affirmative speaker are recorded in the column headed 1A. This speaker's rebuttal arguments are recorded in the column headed 1AR. The same system of recording is used for all of the affirmative and negative speakers, the number of speakers depending on the kind of formal debate being used. An illustration of the sheet used in the Issue Summary Method is shown below.

It is worth noting that many trial judges and attorneys use a similar method as they record the progress of debate in the courtroom. Many business executives also use a similar method as an aid in weighing argu-

THE ISSUE SUMMARY METHOD

Issue	1 A	1 N	2 A	2 N	1 NR	1 AR	2 NR	2 AR
I. xxx	xxx	xxx		xxx		xxx	xxx	
II. xxx	xxx	xxx	xxx					xxx
III. xxx	xxx		xxx	xxx	xxx			xxx
IV. xxx		xxx	xxx	xxx			xxx	
V. xxx			xxx	xxx		xxx	xxx	xxx
VI. xxx			xxx	xxx	xxx		xxx	xxx

From *Argumentation and Debate*, by Austin J. Freeley, © 1961 by Wadsworth Publishing. Reprinted with permission.

ments in favor or against a corporate policy being considered.

THE ORAL CRITIQUE

In some formal debates the judge will deliver an *oral critique* based on the notes and other methods of judging used during the debate. The judge will take several minutes to review this information before making an oral critique. An effective oral critique will accomplish the following:

1. Review the progress of the debate
2. Cite examples of effective use of the principles of argumentation and debate
3. Offer suggestions for improvement
4. Cite the most important factors in arriving at a decision
5. Announce the decision

When the decision is in your team's favor, it is good to know exactly how the judge reached this decision. If you have lost, it is also good to know why, and also how you can best improve your techniques so you will have a better chance of winning next time.

THE BALLOT

The most common form of reporting decisions in a formal debate is the ballot. One reason this is preferred is that it provides a permanent record of the event. Sometimes an oral critique is given along with presentation of the ballot. Or sometimes a judge may be asked to prepare a written critique along with the ballot. An effective ballot will provide all of the the following information:

1. Record the decision on the debate
2. Record quality-rating points on important criteria for each debater
3. Record the rank of each debater
4. For each team, provide a record of the achievements of each of the participants
5. Provide a permanent record of the results

A ballot that meets these requirements is shown on pages 90 and 91. The top portion is used for the permanent record of the school sponsoring the debate. The middle section is given to the affirmative team at the conclusion of the debate, and the bottom section is given to the negative team. These sections report on the quality of the participants' debating performance in the following areas: analysis—plan of case; knowledge and evidence; reasoning, inferences; adapting to opposing case; skill in refutation; speaking skill.

Each debater is ranked in order of excellence by placing 1, 2, 3, or 4 in the parentheses to the right of the debater's name in all three sections of the form. The number 1 indicates the most effective, 4 the least effective. However, in judging the quality of debating for each of the six phases of the debate, the numbering system used for points is: 1—poor; 2—fair; 3—good; 4—excellent; and 5—superior. The team with the highest points is judged the winner.

DIRECT-CLASH
DEBATING BALLOT

Another type of ballot used in formal debating that could also be used in informal debates is the Direct-Clash Debating Ballot, shown on page 92. This ballot is based on how the opposing teams, affirmative and negative, handle direct clashes of opinion. In other words,

OFFICIAL JUDGING FORM

Classification _____ Round _____ Date _____ Judge _____

Aff. Team _____ vs. Neg. Team _____

	Rank	Points			Rank	Points
1st Aff. Speaker _____	(___)	(___)	1st Neg. Speaker _____		(___)	(___)
2nd Aff. Speaker _____	(___)	(___)	2nd Neg. Speaker _____		(___)	(___)
Team Totals (Points)	Aff. _____			Neg. _____		

In my opinion, the more effective debating was done by the

_____ team from _____ _____ _____
       (Aff. or Neg.)   (Name of College)   (Signed)   (Judge)

TO THE JUDGE: Please fill in the entire ballot. Please do not render a decision as a tie. The debaters will greatly appreciate it if you will write your comments on the back of the appropriate section below. These sections will be given to the teams as indicated. The above section is for our files.

Speaker's Norms: 7 or below poor; 8 to 13 fair; 14 to 19 good; 20 to 25 excellent; 26 to 30 superior.

Team Norms: 14 or below poor; 15 to 26 fair; 27 to 38 good; 39 to 50 excellent; 51 to 60 superior.

FOR THE AFFIRMATIVE TEAM

Aff. _____ vs. Neg. _____ Judge _____

I. _Quality of Debating_

NOTE: Assign to each speaker the _points_ which best describe your evaluation of the quality of debating done in each of the six phases.
1—poor; 2—fair; 3—good; 4—excellent; 5—superior.

	Affirmative										Negative									
	Rank						Rank					Rank						Rank			
	1. (___) 2. (___)						1. (___) 2. (___)					1. (___) 2. (___)						1. (___) 2. (___)			
	1	2	3	4	5		1	2	3	4	5	1	2	3	4	5		1	2	3	4	5
Analysis—plan of case																					
Knowledge and Evidence																					
Reasoning, inferences																					
Adapting to opposing case																					
Skill in refutation																					
Speaking skill																					

Speaker's Totals (points) _____ Aff. _____ Neg. _____

Team Totals (points) _____

II. Rank of Debaters

NOTE: Please rank debaters in order of their excellence by placing 1, 2, 3, or 4 in the parentheses to the right of the debater's name in all three sections of this form. (1 indicates the most effective; 4 the least effective)

III. Decision

The more effective debating was done by: _____

FOR THE NEGATIVE TEAM

Aff. _____ vs. Neg. _____ Judge _____

I. Quality of Debating

NOTE: Assign to each speaker the *points* which best describe your evaluation of the quality of debating done in each of the six phases.
1—p o o r ; 2—fair; 3—good; 4—excellent; 5—superior.

	Affirmative		Negative	
	Rank	Rank	Rank	Rank
	1. ( )	2. ( )	1. ( )	2. ( )
	1 2 3 4 5	1 2 3 4 5	1 2 3 4 5	1 2 3 4 5
Analysis—plan of case				
Knowledge and Evidence				
Reasoning, inferences				
Adapting to opposing case				
Skill in refutation				
Speaking skill				

Speaker's Totals (points) _____ Aff. _____ Neg. _____

Team Totals (points) _____

II. Rank of Debaters

NOTE: Please rank debaters in order of their excellence by placing 1, 2, 3, or 4 in the parentheses to the right of the debater's name in all three sections of this form. (1 indicates the most effective; 4 the least effective)

III. Decision

The more effective debating was done by: _____

OFFICIAL JUDGING FORM FOR DIRECT–CLASH DEBATES

Classification _____ Round _____ Date _____ Judge _____

Aff. Team _____ vs. Neg. Team _____

No. of clashes won: Aff. _____ Neg. _____

Therefore, the winner of this debate was the_____
                                               (Aff. or Neg.)

team from: _____ Signed: _____
           (Name of College)   (Judge)

FOR THE AFFIRMATIVE TEAM

Aff. _____ vs. Neg. _____ Judge _____

Clash 1 _____   _____

Clash 2 _____   _____

Clash 3 _____   _____

Clash 4 _____   _____

Clash 5 _____   _____

No. of clashes won: Aff. _____ Neg. _____

Decision won by: _____

FOR THE NEGATIVE TEAM

Aff. _____ vs. Neg. _____ Judge _____

Clash 1 _____   _____

Clash 2 _____   _____

Clash 3 _____   _____

Clash 4 _____   _____

Clash 5 _____   _____

No. of clashes won: Aff. _____ Neg. _____

Decision won by: _____

From *Argumentation and Debate*, by Austin J. Freeley, © 1961 by Wadsworth Publishing. Reprinted with permission.

how effectively they are able to handle specific arguments, those offered as evidence by one side and opposed by the other.

Still another ballot, this one for use by the audience, is called the Official Audience Shift-of-Opinion Ballot, shown on this page. This could also be used in informal debating to help determine how effective one team or the other is in confirming or changing the audience's opinion about the proposition being debated. It also adds an extra challenge to those involved in a debate to win the audience, as well as the judge, to their side. It is a good test of effective conviction and persuasion.

FORMAL DEBATES

9

Both formal and informal debating have many characteristics in common. There are two opposing teams, the affirmative and the negative, and representatives of each team present the opening statements or constructive speeches, and the rebuttals. Time limits are set for the opening statements, preparation for the rebuttals, and the rebuttals.

All of the techniques needed for effective informal debating are the same techniques used in formal debates. The person who judges either informal or formal debating will use essentially the same standards in reaching a decision. However, there are important differences.

For one thing, there are usually more team members on each side in an informal debate. However, only those members chosen by each team will make the opening statements and the rebuttals. In formal debating, if there are two members on each team, each of them will make an opening statement or constructive speech, as well as a rebuttal. The time limits allowed in

informal debating for opening statement, rebuttal preparation, and rebuttal are not rigid. They will vary according to rules set down by the instructor. In formal debating, the time limits are determined by the type of formal
debate being used.

The judging in formal debating also differs in that
usually the judge will have a specific set of standards to
use in arriving at a decision. These are usually indicated
on the ballot used by the judge in formal debating. They
are also indicated in rules that the judge is expected to
follow for a particular kind of formal debate.

STANDARD DEBATING

There are many types of *formal educational debates*,
some of which will be discussed in this chapter. In general, they have three elements in common: (1) both
sides must have an equal number of speakers; (2) both
sides must have an equal amount of time; and (3) the
affirmative side must speak first and last. The standard
type of debating, the one most widely used in the United States, is structured as follows:

STANDARD DEBATING

First affirmative speech	10 minutes
First negative speech	10 minutes
Second affirmative speech	10 minutes
Second negative speech	10 minutes
First negative rebuttal	5 minutes
First affirmative rebuttal	5 minutes
Second negative rebuttal	5 minutes
Second affirmative rebuttal	5 minutes

DIRECT-CLASH DEBATE

Among the interesting variations in formal debating is
the *Direct-Clash Debate.* In this type of debating the

judge takes an active role in the conduct of the debate. In the version designed for two-person teams, the following format is used:

DIRECT CLASH DEBATE

1. *Definition and Analysis*
   a. The first affirmative defines terms and outlines the affirmative team's basic position on the proposition, stating the issues that the affirmative team wants to debate. *5 minutes*
   b. The first negative either accepts or rejects the affirmative's definition and analysis and the proposed issues to be debated. The negative has the option of proposing additional issues to be debated. If a counter plan is proposed, it must be presented as an issue at this time. *5 minutes*
   c. The judge may rule on the issues at this time.

2. *First Clash*
   a. The second affirmative presents a single issue that he or she believes vital to the affirmative's case. *4 minutes*
   b. The second negative attempts to disprove the preceding speech. *3 minutes*
   c. The first affirmative reestablishes the second affirmative's argument. *3 minutes*
   d. The first negative attempts to disprove the argument. *3 minutes*
   e. When this clash ends, the judge records the winner on his or her ballot and announces the decision.

3. *Second Clash*
   a. The second negative presents a single issue. *4 minutes*

b. The second affirmative attempts to disprove the argument. *3 minutes*
c. The first negative reestablishes the issue. *3 minutes*
d. The first affirmative attempts to disprove the argument. *3 minutes*
e. The judge records the winner on his or her ballot and announces the decision.

4. *Third Clash*
   This clash follows the same pattern as the others, but this time the first affirmative presents a single issue. The judge announces his or her decision and whether another clash is needed.

5. *Fourth Clash*
   Again the same pattern is followed, with the first negative initiating the issue.

6. *Fifth Clash*
   Again the same pattern is followed, with the second affirmative initiating the issue.

In this style of formal debating, when each person or team member clashes on a specific issue, only that particular issue may be argued, not the entire proposition. Also, after the definition and analysis stage, the judge has the option of playing an active role in the conduct of the debate.

However, if the judge believes that the definition of terms and statement of basic positions have been expressed clearly and convincingly, the debate may be allowed to continue without direction from him or her. Sometimes, however, there may be a strong disagreement over terms. When that happens the judge may rule that the first clash must deal with this problem.

When the statement of basic positions of both or

either teams is not clear, the judge may take charge by stating the issues that should be debated. He or she will also determine the order in which they will be debated. The judge may also take charge when a speaker evades a point in one of the clashes or answers so inadequately that the position of the speaker's team on that issue is destroyed. When that happens the judge may stop the clash.

This type of debate is usually limited to five clashes, but under the rules of Direct-Clash Debate the debate continues until one team has won three clashes. This means there must be at least three clashes but no more than five.

THE HECKLING DEBATE

The *Heckling Debate* follows the pattern of legislative debate as it is practiced in state legislatures or in the House of Representatives or Senate. This is how it is structured:

First affirmative	10 minutes
Heckling by first negative	
First negative	10 minutes
Heckling by second affirmative	
Second affirmative	10 minutes
Heckling by second negative	
Second negative	10 minutes
Heckling by first affirmative	
First negative rebuttal	5 minutes
Heckling by first affirmative	
First affirmative rebuttal	5 minutes
Heckling by second negative	
Second negative rebuttal	5 minutes
Heckling by second affirmative	
Second affirmative rebuttal	5 minutes
Heckling by first negative	

In a Heckling Debate, speakers on both sides of the question can be interrupted by members of the opposing team. This must be done formally, however, by asking, "Will the speaker yield for a question?" The speaker, of course, has no choice. He or she must yield. However, the question must be short and be directly related to the argument or evidence the speaker is discussing.

During the constructive speech (opening statement) the heckler may interrupt the speaker four times. This can occur any time after the third minute of the speech and before the eighth minute. During the rebuttal speech, the heckler may interrupt twice—any time after the first minute of the rebuttal and prior to the fourth minute.

In some ways the Heckling Debate is similar to the cross-examination style of debating used by law students. The responses to the questions asked by the hecklers are designed to be used later by the hecklers, either to advance their own case or challenge their opponents' case. However, the judge will penalize a heckler if he or she asks questions that are too long or irrelevant. Also, this type of debate requires very careful timing. The timekeeper in this style of debate is therefore instructed to announce, at the designated time, "Heckling may begin" or "heckling must cease."

LINCOLN–DOUGLAS DEBATE

The *Lincoln–Douglas Debate* is named in honor of the famous duo who used this form to debate the slavery issue in 1858 and 1859. Though not as popular in schools as other forms of debate, it provides good training in argumentation. It is often used by political groups. When the first televised presidential debates were held in 1960, the Lincoln–Douglas Debate format served as a guide. The timing for radio or television debates will vary according to preset requirements. For classroom use, however, this type of debate is usually structured as follows:

LINCOLN-DOUGLAS DEBATE

Affirmative	10 minutes
Negative	15 minutes
Affirmative	5 minutes

THE DEBATE-FORUM

The *Debate-Forum*, like the Lincoln–Douglas Debate, lends itself well to television and is often used during political campaigns of national importance, such as the presidential election campaign. The most common format is that of the standard debate discussed at the beginning of this chapter. This is followed by a "forum" period, during which time members of the audience are invited to address questions to the debaters.

In the Debate–Forum the constructive speeches or opening statements are shorter, and may be only six minutes long. The rebuttal speeches may be limited to three minutes. The time allowed will depend on the number of debaters.

By shortening the time for constructive and rebuttal speeches, and allowing twenty minutes for questions from the audience, this type of debate can be scheduled for an hour, which is well-adapted to television requirements.

A chairperson or moderator will be designated to oversee the debate and, in particular, the forum portion. It will be his or her responsibility to prevent a few questioners from monopolizing the forum period. The chairperson must also discourage speeches from the floor that are disguised as questions. Wordy or vague questions, or those difficult to hear, must be restated so that the entire audience can hear them. It is also the chair-person's responsibility to make sure the debating process and forum period move along at a good pace and stick to the topic.

DEBATING IN YOUR STATE

If you and other classmates are interested in organizing a debate team or finding out about educational debates scheduled in your state, contact the president of the state Forensic Association. This person will be able to provide you with information about both state and national debates.

Your state's Forensic Association will also be able to provide you and your instructor with details on how a debate team can be organized, and how it can meet Forensic Association standards. Another good source of information about debates and debating teams is your state's School Principals Association.

GLOSSARY

Affirmative Team. The team that argues in favor of the proposition.

Analyzing the Proposition. Studying all the arguments and evidence to find the main issues in favor of or against the proposition.

Arguments. Facts, authoritative statements, other evidence and reasoning in favor of or against the proposition.

Argumentation. To show the likelihood, through arguments, examples, evidence, and persuasion that a given proposition is true or false. A synonym for debate.

Argument from Analogy. A technique in which a debater infers that a certain fact known to be true of A, is more likely to be true of B, if B resembles A in certain essential characteristics or conditions.

Ballot. In formal debate the most common form of reporting decisions, with points and ratings assigned by the judge to each affirmative and negative team member, as well as to the team as a whole. The top portion is used for the permanent record of the school sponsoring the debate; the middle portion is given to the affirmative team, and the bottom portion to the negative team.

Case. A set of reasons, arguments, supporting facts and other evidence, presented in favor of or against the proposition.

Case Summary Method. A procedure in which a judge records an outline of the cases presented by the affirmative and negative teams, using sheets of paper divided by a vertical line. The issues, arguments, and evidence presented by the affirmative team are recorded on one side, and by the negative team on the other side.

Counter-Argument. An opposing argument put forward by one team against an argument presented by the opposing team.

Debate-Forum. Standard debate followed by a forum period in which members of the audience are invited to address questions to the debaters. A chairperson or moderator oversees both the debate and the forum portion.

Deductive Reasoning. A method of logic in which you begin with a generalization and thereby reach a specific conclusion.

Direct-Clash Debate. A form of debate in which affirmative and negative teams clash on specific issues until one team has won three clashes and is declared the winner. The judge may take an active role in this type of formal debate.

Errors in Reasoning. Faulty logic, incomplete or unsubstantiated evidence, and fallacies that weaken or destroy a debater's arguments.

Evidence. Facts, examples, statements of authority, and other information used by a debater to

strengthen his or her arguments to prove or disprove the proposition being debated.

Fallacies. Errors in reasoning or arguments that are
unsuccessful in proving (1) what caused certain
conditions to exist or (2) that certain conditions will
have a particular result.

Flowsheet. One of the tools of debate used to record
arguments, counter-arguments, and evidence put
forth by a debating team and its opponents. By
using shorthand, a team is able to record a great
deal of information in a limited amount of time for
possible use in rebuttal speeches.

Formal Educational Debate. A form of debate that
includes the following requirements: (1) both sides
must have an equal number of speakers; (2) both
sides must have an equal amount of time.

Heckling Debate. A type of formal debate designed to
simulate legislative debate as practiced in the state
legislature or in the House of Representatives or
Senate. Speakers on both sides of the proposition
can be questioned by members of the opposing
team during their speeches, with limits set for the
number of questions, and the time in which they can
be asked.

Inconsistencies. Elements of reasoning and argument
that are unsound because they ignore, omit, misin-
terpret, or withhold important evidence or facts.

Inductive Reasoning. A method of logic in which you
begin with specific facts or examples and thereby
reach a generalization or conclusion.

Introducing Personalities. Attacking your opponents
personally. Not recommended.

Issue Summary Method. A judging procedure in which
the judge uses sheets of paper with columns indi-
cating the issues raised, which speakers raise
them, and when they are challenged by the opposition.

Lincoln–Douglas Debate. A two-person formal debate named in honor of the famous duo who used this form to debate the slavery issue in 1858 and 1859.

Logic. That part of argumentation concerned with the reasoning process.

Main Issues. The major evidence used by affirmative and negative teams to prove or disprove the proposition.

Negative Team. The team that argues against the proposition.

Opening Statement. A constructive speech that each side uses to begin the debate.

Oral Critique. A procedure in which the judge criticizes the debate orally, based on notes and other methods of judging she or he has used during the debate.

Proposition. The statement on which a debate is based.

Rebuttal. The response to your opponents' arguments and counter-arguments.

Reductio Ad Absurdum. A technique used to reduce an opponent's arguments to absurdity.

Shorthand. A system of taking notes in which unnecessary words are omitted and some necessary words are shortened or abbreviated. It may include symbols, acronyms (words formed from the initial letters of a name, e.g., UN = United Nations), and other word substitution techniques. To be effective it must be legible and accurate.

Subordinate Issues. Issues important to the arguments presented but secondary to the main issues.

Unified Attack. A method of attack or presentation in which all of a debater's arguments and evidence fit together as a whole.

Weight of Evidence. The sum total of all the evidence presented to prove or disprove the proposition.

DEBATE TOPICS AND SOURCES

NOTE: This list of topics and sources doesn't begin to cover the almost infinite number of subjects that would be appropriate and meaningful for both informal and formal debate. Its main intent is to provide a beginning point of suggestions and ideas to explore before selecting a proposition to debate.

ABORTION

Batchelor, Edward, Jr., ed. *Abortion: The Moral Issues.* New York: Pilgrim Press, 1982.

Dolan, Edward F, Jr. *Matters of Life and Death.* New York: Franklin Watts, 1982.

Mother Teresa. "A Nobel Laureate Speaks in Defense of Unborn Life." *Christ Today.* 29:62–3, Sept. 6, 1985.

Petchesky, Rosalind P. *Abortion and Woman's Choice: The State, Sexuality, and Reproductive Freedom.* Boston: Northeastern University Press, 1985.

"Senate Abortion Debate." *MacNeil/Lehrer NewsHour.* Transcript #1797, Aug. 17, 1982.

Spake, A. "The Propaganda War Over Abortion." *Ms Magazine,* 14:90-2+, July, 1985.

ACID RAIN

"Acid Rain." *MacNeil/Lehrer NewsHour.* Transcript #2179, Feb. 2, 1984.

"Acid Rain on the Brain." *Mother Earth News.* 94:114, July–August, 1985.

Gay, Kathlyn. *Acid Rain.* New York: Franklin Watts, 1983.

Luoma, Jon R. *Troubled Skies, Troubled Waters: The Story of Acid Rain.* New York: Viking Penguin, Inc., 1984.

Taylor, R.A. "Acid Rain Spreads Its Deadly Sting." *U.S. News and World Report.* Oct. 7, 1985.

Yanarella, Ernest J., and Ihara, Randal H., eds. *The Acid Rain Debate: Scientific, Economic, and Political Dimensions.* Boulder, Colorado: Westview Press, 1985

AFRO–AMERICAN OPPORTUNITIES

Glasgow, Douglas C. *The Black Underclass: Poverty, Unemployment, and Entrapment of Ghetto Youth.* New York: Random House, 1981.

Green, C. "Putting Your Career in High Gear." *Black Enterprise.* 16:63, September, 1985.

Lewis, Jerry M., and Looney, John G. *The Long Struggle: Well-Functioning Working Class Black Families.* New York: Brunner, Mazel, Inc., 1983.

Loury, G.C. "Beyond Civil Rights." *New Republic.* 193:22-5, Oct. 7, 1985.

Pascoe, Elaine. *Racial Prejudice.* New York: Franklin Watts, 1985.

"State of Black America," *MacNeil/Lehrer NewsHour. Transcript #1646, Jan. 18, 1982.*

ANTINUCLEAR MOVEMENTS

Andrews, Elaine K. *Civil Defense in the Nuclear Age.* New York: Franklin Watts, 1985.

Baer, B.L. "Pageant and Protest." *Commonweal.* 112:453–4, Sept. 6, 1985.

Dougherty, James E., et al. *Ethics, Deterrence, and National Security.* Elmsford, New York: Pergamon Press, 1985.

Farren, Pat, ed. *What Will It Take to Prevent Nuclear War?* Cambridge, Massachusetts: Schenkman Books, Inc., 1983.

"Nuclear Freeze Issue." *MacNeil/Lehrer NewsHour. Transcript #1848, Oct. 27, 1982.*

Peck, K. "First Strike, You're Out: An Interview with Daniel Ellsberg." *The Progressive,* 49:30–5, July, 1985.

Taylor, L.B., Jr. *The Nuclear Arms Race.* New York: Franklin Watts, 1982.

FAMILY VIOLENCE

Davis, Diane. *Something Is Wrong At My House.* Seattle: Parenting Press, 1985.

"Family Violence and Unemployment." *MacNeil/Lehrer NewsHour.* Transcript #1900, Jan. 7, 1983.

Kratcoski, P.C. "Attacking Family Violence." *USA Today.* 114:98, September, 1985.

Mintie, D. "Family Violence: When People Hurt the Ones They Love." *U.S. Catholic.* 50:36–40, February, 1985.

Siegal, Mark A., et al, eds. *Domestic Violence: No Longer Behind the Curtains.* Plano, Texas: Instructional Aids, Inc., 1985.

POVERTY

Claypool, Jane. *Unemployment.* New York: Franklin Watts, 1983.

Galbraith, J.K. "How to Get the Poor Off Our Conscience." *The Humanist.* 45:5–9+, September–October, 1985.

MacGregor, Susanne. *The Politics of Poverty.* White Plains, New York: Longman, Inc., 1982.

"Poverty Rise." *MacNeil/Lehrer NewsHour.* Transcript #2059, Aug. 18, 1983.

Sehgal, E. "Employment Problems and Their Effect on Family Income." *Monthly Labor Review.* 108:42–3, August, 1985.

Williams, Terry, and Kornblum, William. *Growing Up Poor.* Lexington, Massachusetts: Lexington Books, 1985.

PRISONS

Budgen, M. "A Crusader for Convicts." *MacLean's.* 98:6+, Aug. 5, 1985.

"Bulging Prisons—State by State." *U.S. News and World Report.* 99:10, Sept. 23, 1985.

Cordilla, Ann. *The Making of An Inmate.* Cambridge, Massachusetts: Schenkman Books, 1983.

"Kentucky Women's Prison." *MacNeil/Lehrer NewsHour.* Transcript #1780, July 23, 1982.

Murton, Thomas O. *The Dilemma of Prison Reform.* New York: Irvington Publishers, 1982.

SCHOOL PRAYER

McMillan, Richard C. *Religion in Public Schools: An Introduction.* Macon, Georgia: Mercer University Press, 1984.

"The Mormon Example," *America.* 153:181, Oct. 5, 1985.

Rugh, Charles E. *Moral Training in the Public Schools.* Philadelphia: Richard West, 1980.

"School Prayer." *MacNeil/Lehrer NewsHour.* Transcript #1823, Sept. 22, 1982.

TELEVISION VIOLENCE

Cantor, Muriel G. *Prime-Time Television: Content and Control.* Beverly Hills, California: Sage Publications, 1980.

Chaze, W.L. "What America Thinks of TV." *U.S. News and World Report.* 98:67–8, May 13, 1985.

Cheney, Glenn Alan. *Television in American Society.* New York: Franklin Watts, 1983.

James, Clive. *Glued to the Box: Television Criticism from the Observer, 1979–82.* Salem, New Hampshire: Merrimack Publishers Circle, 1983.

"TV: The View from the Couch." *Vogue.* 175:332-7, February, 1985.

"TV Violence." *MacNeil/Lehrer NewsHour*, Transcript #1911, Jan. 24, 1983.

TOBACCO USE

Balfour, D.J. *Nicotine and the Tobacco Smoking Habit.* Elmsford, New York: Pergamon Press, 1984.

Fitzgerald, Jim. *The Joys of Smoking Cigarettes.* New York: Holt, Rinehart & Winston, 1983.

Kohn, A. "Smoking Gun." *The Nation.* 241:36–7, July 20–27, 1985.

"Tobacco Hearings." *MacNeil/Lehrer NewsHour.* Transcript #1955, March 3, 1983.

White, L. "Suing the Tobacco Companies." *Saturday Evening Post.* 257:58-61+, July–August, 1985.

TOXIC WASTES

"A Poisoned Town." *MacNeil/Lehrer NewsHour.* Transcript #1904, Jan. 13, 1983.

Berle, P.A.A. "The Toxic Tornado." *Audubon.* 87:4, November, 1985.

Cook, J. "Risky Business." *Forbes.* 136:106–7+, Dec. 2, 1985.

Cooper, M.G., ed. *Risk: Man-Made Hazards to Man.* New York: Oxford University Press, 1985.

Knowledge Unlimited Staff. *Toxic Wastes: The Fouling of America.* Madison, Wisconsin: Knowledge Unlimited, 1984.

Stwertka, Eve and Albert. *Industrial Pollution: Poisoning Our World.* New York: Franklin Watts, 1981.

Weiss, Malcolm E. *Toxic Waste: Cleanup or Coverup?* New York: Franklin Watts, 1984.

WOMEN'S STATUS IN THE U.S.

Brown, Rusty *Women As We See Ourselves.* Indianapolis: News Books International, 1984.

Christopher, M. "The Struggle Against 'Job Segregation' ". *Scholastic Update.* 118:4–5, Nov. 29, 1985.

Claypool, Jane. *The Worker in America.* New York: Franklin Watts, 1985.

Duley-Morrow, Margot, and Edwards, Mary I., eds. *The Cross-Cultural Study of Women: A Comprehensive Guide.* New York: Feminist Press at the City University of New York, 1985.

"ERA, Abortion, and the GOP." *MacNeil/Lehrer NewsHour.* Transcript #1249, July 10, 1980.

Simpson, P. "The Return of 'Barefoot and Pregnant' ". *Working Woman.* 10:48+, December 1985.

SPECIAL NOTE: The above bibliography includes transcripts of debates conducted on the *MacNeil/Lehrer*

NewsHour, televised five times a week on public television stations. For information about transcripts available, write to *MacNeil/Lehrer NewsHour,* Box 345, New York, NY 10101.

Other rich sources of debate transcripts include *The Firing Line,* a continuing weekly series of debates on public television and radio, hosted by William F. Buckley, Jr., noted writer, speaker, and debater. For a listing of debate transcripts available, write to Southern Educational Communications Association, 928 Woodrow St., P.O. Box 5966, Columbia, SC 29250.

A high point in presidential election years since 1976 have been the forums and debates sponsored by the League of Women Voters Education Fund. For information about transcripts available write to The League of Women Voters of the United States, 1730 M St. NW, Washington, DC 20036.

Another useful source for books on debating topics is the "Opposing Viewpoints" series published by Greenhaven Press, 577 Shoreview Park Road, St. Paul, MN 55112.

SUGGESTIONS FOR FURTHER READING

Foster, William Trufant. *Argumentation and Debating.* 2nd revised edition. Boston: Houghton Mifflin, 1932.

Freeley, Austin J. *Argumentation and Debate.* 5th edition, Belmont, California: Wadsworth Publishing Co., 1981.

Gulley, Halbert E., and Biddle, Phillips R. *Essentials of Debate.* New York: Holt, Rinehart & Winston, 1972.

Jaffa, Harry V. *Crisis of The House Divided.* An Interpretation of the Issues in the Lincoln–Douglas Debates. Chicago: University of Chicago Press, 1982.

Johannsen, Robert W. *The Lincoln–Douglas Debates of 1858.* New York: Oxford University Press, 1965.

ANNUAL NATIONAL DEBATE COMPETITIONS

OPEN TO HIGH SCHOOL STUDENTS

Annual Debate Tournament of the Catholic Forensic League. Open to contestants from all public and private schools. Held at various sites in the United States. For information write to Richard Gaudette, Secretary-Treasurer, Catholic Forensic League, Natick High School, Natick, MA 01760.

Harvard Debate Tournament. Held in February at Harvard University, Cambridge, Massachusetts. For information write to Dallas Perkins, Harvard Debate Tournament, Quincy House, Harvard University, Cambridge, MA.

National Speech and Debate Tournament. Sponsored by the National Forensic League, held in June at various host high schools in the United States. For information write to the National Forensic League, Ripon, Wisconsin.

Tournament of Champions. Held annually in May at the University of Kentucky in Lexington, sponsored by the University of Kentucky Debate Association. For information write to the Director of Debate, University of Kentucky, Lexington, KY.

INDEX

ABOUT THE AUTHOR

Robert E. Dunbar is the author of *The Heart and Circulatory System, Heredity, Zoology Careers, Mental Retardation*, and the science fiction novel *Into Jupiter's World*, all for Franklin Watts. In addition to meeting commitments as a professional writer, Mr. Dunbar is a part-time teacher and performs occasionally as an actor and singer. He has two children and lives and works in Damariscotta, Maine.

DATE DUE

MAR 2 2		
Sept 17		

DEMCO 38-297